THE STATUE OF LIBERTY WASN'T MADE TO WELCOME IMMIGRANTS

EXPOSING MYTHS ABOUT US LANDMARKS

BY THERESE M. SHEA

Gareth Stevens
PUBLISHING

Please visit our website, www.garethstevens.com. For a free color catalog of all our high-quality books, call toll free 1-800-542-2595 or fax 1-877-542-2596.

Library of Congress Cataloging-in-Publication Data

Names: Shea, Therese, author.
Title: The Statue of Liberty wasn't made to welcome immigrants : exposing myths about U.S. landmarks / Therese M. Shea.
Description: New York : Gareth Stevens Publishing, 2020. | Series: Exposed! More myths about American history | Includes index.
Identifiers: LCCN 2018049568| ISBN 9781538237588 (pbk.) | ISBN 9781538237601 (library bound) | ISBN 9781538237595 (6 pack)
Subjects: LCSH: Statue of Liberty (New York, N.Y.)–Juvenile literature. | Statue of Liberty National Monument (N.Y. and N.J.)–Juvenile literature. | New York (N.Y.)–Buildings, structures, etc.–Juvenile literature. | United States–History–Errors, inventions, etc.–Juvenile literature.
Classification: LCC F128.64.L6 S497 2020 | DDC 974.7/1–dc23
LC record available at https://lccn.loc.gov/2018049568

First Edition

Published in 2020 by
Gareth Stevens Publishing
111 East 14th Street, Suite 349
New York, NY 10003

Copyright © 2020 Gareth Stevens Publishing

Designer: Sarah Liddell
Editor: Therese Shea

Photo credits: Cover, p. 1 (harbor) Hohum/Wikimedia Commons; cover, pp. 1 (statue), 13 photo courtesy of Library of Congress; background texture used throughout IS MODE/Shutterstock.com; ripped newspaper used throughout STILLFX/Shutterstock.com; photo corners used throughout Carolyn Franks/Shutterstock.com; p. 5 (inset) Life In Pixels/Shutterstock.com; p. 5 (map) Armita/Shutterstock.com; p. 7 (main) Massimo Salesi/Shutterstock.com; p. 7 (inset) Bettmann/Contributor/Bettmann/Getty Images; p. 9 Tono Balaguer/Shutterstock.com; p. 11 (main) Jorge Salcedo/Shutterstock.com; p. 11 (inset) ESB Basic/Shutterstock.com; p. 15 Anton Foltin/Shutterstock.com; p. 17 critterbiz/Shutterstock.com; p. 19 (main) ventdusud/Shutterstock.com; p. 19 (inset) Michael D Lewis/Shutterstock.com; p. 21 (statue) Howcheng/Wikimedia Commons; p. 21 (photo) Alexis Jazz/Wikimedia Commons; p. 23 Danita Delimont/Gallo Images/Getty Images; p. 25 amolson7/Shutterstock.com; p. 27 f11photo/Shutterstock.com; p. 29 (main) CPQ/Shutterstock.com; p. 29 (inset) Jason Patrick Ross/Shutterstock.com.

CPSIA compliance information: Batch #CS19GS: For further information contact Gareth Stevens, New York, New York at 1-800-542-2595.

CONTENTS

Words in the glossary appear in **bold** type the first time they are used in the text.

BUSTING MYTHS

Did you ever believe something was true for a long time—and suddenly find out it wasn't? You were probably very surprised. Maybe you decided to check your facts again with other sources. But some **myths** are even in history books. That makes finding the truth even trickier!

In this book, you'll look into well-known myths about American landmarks and discover the truth behind them. Once you learn the facts, tell others so these myths don't keep spreading. Are you ready to bust some myths?

WASHINGTON MONUMENT

FACT-FINDING MISSION: US LANDMARKS!

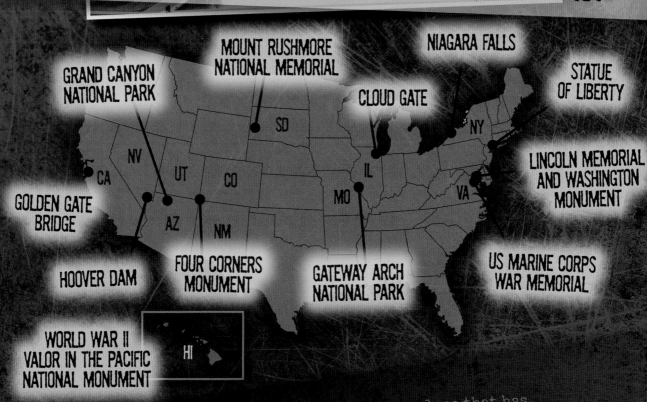

MOUNT RUSHMORE NATIONAL MEMORIAL

NIAGARA FALLS

GRAND CANYON NATIONAL PARK

CLOUD GATE

STATUE OF LIBERTY

GOLDEN GATE BRIDGE

LINCOLN MEMORIAL AND WASHINGTON MONUMENT

HOOVER DAM

FOUR CORNERS MONUMENT

GATEWAY ARCH NATIONAL PARK

US MARINE CORPS WAR MEMORIAL

WORLD WAR II VALOR IN THE PACIFIC NATIONAL MONUMENT

SD · NV · CA · UT · CO · AZ · NM · IL · MO · NY · VA · HI

A landmark is a building, monument, or place that has importance. It's usually easy to recognize. This map pinpoints US landmarks we'll be visiting in this book. Get ready for a cross-country, myth-busting journey!

5

LADY LIBERTY

THE MYTH: THE STATUE OF LIBERTY WAS CREATED TO WELCOME IMMIGRANTS TO THE UNITED STATES.

THE FACTS:

The Statue of Liberty was created as a symbol, or sign, of the friendship between the United States and France.

It was first completed in France in 1885, and then taken apart, shipped to the United States, and reconstructed in New York Harbor.

Between 1892 and 1924, more than 12 million immigrants saw the statue as they entered the United States through Ellis Island. It became a welcoming symbol to them.

"GIVE ME YOUR TIRED, YOUR POOR, . . ."

A poem added to the Statue of Liberty's **pedestal** sealed its connection with immigration. "The New Colossus," by Emma Lazarus, welcomed to American shores all those who needed a new home.

THE NEW COLOSSUS.

NOT LIKE THE BRAZEN GIANT OF GREEK FAME,
WITH CONQUERING LIMBS ASTRIDE FROM LAND TO LAND
HERE AT OUR SEA-WASHED, SUNSET GATES SHALL STAND
A MIGHTY WOMAN WITH A TORCH, WHOSE FLAME
IS THE IMPRISONED LIGHTNING, AND HER NAME
MOTHER OF EXILES. FROM HER BEACON-HAND
GLOWS WORLD-WIDE WELCOME; HER MILD EYES COMMAND
THE AIR-BRIDGED HARBOR THAT TWIN CITIES FRAME.
"KEEP ANCIENT LANDS, YOUR STORIED POMP!"
    CRIES SHE
WITH SILENT LIPS. "GIVE ME YOUR TIRED, YOUR
    POOR,
YOUR HUDDLED MASSES YEARNING TO BREATHE FREE,
THE WRETCHED REFUSE OF YOUR TEEMING SHORE.
SEND THESE, THE HOMELESS, TEMPEST-TOST TO ME,
I LIFT MY LAMP BESIDE THE GOLDEN DOOR!"

THIS TABLET, WITH HER SONNET TO THE BARTHOLDI STATUE
OF LIBERTY ENGRAVED UPON IT, IS PLACED UPON THESE WALLS
IN LOVING MEMORY OF
EMMA LAZARUS
BORN IN NEW YORK CITY, JULY 22, 1849
DIED NOVEMBER 19, 1887.

The Statue of Liberty was reconstructed on Bedloe's Island, now Liberty Island, in New York Harbor.

A MAMMOTH MONUMENT

THE WASHINGTON MONUMENT WAS ALWAYS MEANT TO BE AN OBELISK.

THE FACTS:

Actually, the monument was supposed to be an obelisk and much more. The original 1833 design called for a temple-like building with 30 stone columns. An obelisk was to be placed within it. Along with heroic figures of the American Revolution, a statue of George Washington driving a chariot was **designed** for the front.

However, only the obelisk was built. Construction began in 1848 and was finally completed in 1884.

WHAT LIES BENEATH

Many objects are buried at the base of the Washington Monument, including a Bible and copies of the US Constitution and the Declaration of Independence.

The obelisk measures 554 feet 7 inches (169 m) tall. It was the tallest man-made structure in the world for a time.

EYES IN THE BACK OF HIS HEAD

THE MYTH: ON THE LINCOLN MEMORIAL, ANOTHER FACE WAS **SCULPTED** ON THE BACK OF ABRAHAM LINCOLN'S HEAD.

THE FACTS:

At some point, someone thought the hair on the back of the statue's head looked like a face. Others agreed. Some even said it was the face of **Confederate** general Robert E. Lee looking toward his home across the Potomac River! However, there really is no face there.

Another myth about the Lincoln Memorial is that Lincoln's hands are forming sign language. That, too, isn't true.

Construction of the Lincoln Memorial began in 1915.
A completion ceremony was held in 1922.

STEP UP

There are 57 steps leading to the Lincoln Memorial. However, these aren't meant to stand for Lincoln's age when he was killed, like some think. In fact, Lincoln was 56 when he was shot dead in 1865.

11

SO CLOSE, YET SO FAR

THE MYTH: THE FOUR CORNERS MONUMENT STANDS WHERE THE STATES OF ARIZONA, NEW MEXICO, UTAH, AND COLORADO MEET.

THE FACTS:

The Four Corners Monument in the American Southwest is supposed to mark where the four states come together. This place was located in 1875 by a **surveyor** named Chandler Robbins. Robbins had been hired by the US General Land Office (now called the Bureau of Land Management).

However, a later government survey proved that the actual spot where the states meet is about 1,800 feet (549 m) away!

The land surrounding the Four Corners Monument
belongs to Native Americans: the Navajo and Ute peoples.
The landmark is managed by the Navajo.

NATIVE LIFE AT THE CORNERS

The Four Corners visitor center provides many opportunities to learn about native peoples' lives. Visitors can also buy native crafts.

13

A DEADLY DAM?

THE MYTH: WORKERS WHO DIED WHILE MAKING THE HOOVER DAM ON THE COLORADO RIVER ARE STILL BURIED WITHIN IT.

THE FACTS:

Between 1930 and 1936, thousands of people were hired to build the huge dam at the border between Arizona and New Mexico. About 100 died while working on it. However, none are buried within it. Some people think the construction workers themselves made up this myth!

Today, the Hoover Dam is used to control flooding, create electricity, and supply water for farms and for people's homes and businesses.

The Hoover Dam is 726 feet (221 m) high and 1,244 feet (379 m) long. Millions of people visit it each year.

15

A COLOSSAL CARVING

THE MYTH: THE MOUNT RUSHMORE MONUMENT WAS ALWAYS MEANT TO HONOR AMERICAN PRESIDENTS.

THE FACTS:

Actually, the first idea was for a monument in another part of South Dakota's Black Hills, not on Mount Rushmore. And it was to show famous people of the Wild West as well as Native Americans.

The sculptor Gutzon Borglum decided to display four presidents on Mount Rushmore instead. While workers used **chisels** to create the monument, most of the figures were formed with **dynamite**!

Mount Rushmore shows the faces of George Washington, Thomas Jefferson, Theodore Roosevelt, and Abraham Lincoln. Construction in the Black Hills began in 1927 and ended in 1941.

ON STOLEN LAND

In 1980, the US Supreme Court decided that the US government illegally took the Black Hills from the Lakota Sioux people. The Sioux were offered money but said they would rather have the land back.

17

A BIG PAINT JOB

THE MYTH: THE GOLDEN GATE BRIDGE IS PAINTED EACH YEAR FROM ONE END TO THE OTHER.

THE FACTS:

The Golden Gate Bridge is named for its location, over the Golden Gate Strait. This narrow waterway connects San Francisco Bay to the Pacific Ocean. Visitors to San Francisco, California, marvel at the painted bridge.

However, the bridge isn't painted from end to end yearly. Instead, workers look for places where it needs to be repainted and do "touch-ups."

PLENTY OF PAINT

About 5,000 to 10,000 gallons (18,927 to 37,854 l) of paint are used on the bridge each year for touch-ups!

The official color of the Golden Gate Bridge is "international orange."

AN EXTRA HAND?

THE MYTH: THE UNITED STATES MARINE CORPS WAR MEMORIAL FEATURES SIX SOLDIERS—AND 13 HANDS!

THE FACTS:

The Marine Corps War Memorial, commonly called the Iwo Jima Memorial, is located in Arlington, Virginia. The monument shows a group of marines raising the US flag on the Japanese island of Iwo Jima during World War II. It honors marines who have died in service of their country.

Someone started the myth that the sculpture features 13 hands instead of 12. Even the sculptor says that's not true!

The memorial sculpture is based on a photograph that was taken during a battle on Iwo Jima on February 23, 1945.

UNCOMMON
VALOR
WAS A COMMON
VIRTUE

FIDELIS

950-   REVOLUTIONARY WAR 1775-1783 ★ FRENCH NAVAL WAR 1798-1801 ★ TRIPOLI 1801-1805★

OVER THE ARIZONA

THE MYTH: THE MEMORIAL TO THE USS *ARIZONA* CONTAINS OPENINGS THAT STAND FOR A 21-GUN SALUTE FOR THE SOLDIERS WHO DIED ABOARD THE SHIP.

THE FACTS:

On December 7, 1941, Japan attacked a naval base at Pearl Harbor in Hawaii. The battleship USS *Arizona* sank and more than 1,170 crewmen were killed. A steel and concrete memorial was built over the top of the sunken ship.

While there are a number of openings in it, the number doesn't mean anything. However, their shape is meant to look like marines standing guard over the soldiers below.

Visitors to the USS Arizona memorial, called the World War II Valor in the Pacific National Monument, can look through an opening in the floor to see the ship below.

23

AN IMMENSE ARCH

THE MYTH: THE GATEWAY ARCH, ON THE BANKS OF THE MISSISSIPPI RIVER IN ST. LOUIS, MISSOURI, IS TALLER THAN IT IS WIDE.

THE FACTS:

We can blame this myth on our eyes! The Arch is 630 feet (192 m) tall and 630 feet (192 m) wide, but, depending where you stand, it often seems taller than it is wide. The monument is meant to look like a door or gate.

In the 1800s, St. Louis was said to be the gateway to the western part of the country. In fact, Meriwether Lewis and William Clark set out from St. Louis in 1804 to explore the **Louisiana Purchase.**

One of the men who worked on the design for the Gateway Arch recently said it was meant to control the weather! Could this be true—or is it another myth?

The Gateway Arch was completed in 1965. It's the tallest monument in the United States! Visitors can take a ride up the Arch to see the view from the top.

BEAN-FREE

THE MYTH:

IN THE MIDDLE OF THE CITY OF CHICAGO, ILLINOIS, IS A SCULPTURE OF A GIANT BEAN.

THE FACTS:

It may look like a big bean, but the stainless-steel sculpture in Chicago's Millennium Park was actually designed to look like liquid **mercury.** Its special shape is meant to **reflect** the sky above, but people can walk around it and under it to see their own reflections, too.

The sculpture, called Cloud Gate, was constructed between 2004 and 2006.

It may not actually be a sculpture of a bean, but many people still call it "the Bean"!

27

MORE LANDMARKS, MORE MYTHS

Not all American landmarks are man-made. Millions of people travel to see Niagara Falls each year. Some think the water is turned off each night! While this myth seems silly, the fact is that the water flow is cut down each night. Some water is directed to tunnels and carried to power plants that use it to produce electricity.

Sometimes there's just a bit of truth to find behind a myth. Now it's time for you to bust some myths and unearth the facts yourself. The truth is out there!

Niagara Falls is made up of three falls: Horseshoe Falls on the Canadian side and the American Falls and Bridal Veil Falls in the United States.

GRAND CANYON

GRAND CANYON

The Grand Canyon is a natural landmark in northern Arizona. Some facts about this amazing place are crazier than the myths. For example, some canyon rocks are 4 *billion* years old!

29

GLOSSARY

chisel: a metal tool with a straight, flat end used for cutting and shaping wood or stone

Confederate: having to do with the Confederate States of America during the American Civil War (1861–1865)

design: the pattern or shape of something. Also, to create the pattern or shape of something.

dynamite: a powerful explosive

immigrant: one who comes to a country to settle there

Louisiana Purchase: territory of the western United States bought from France

mercury: a silver metal that is liquid at normal temperatures

myth: an idea or story that is believed by many people but that is not true

obelisk: a column of stone with a square base, sides that slope in, and a pyramid on top

pedestal: the base of a column or tall object

reflect: to give back as an image or likeness

sculpt: to create a shape with stone, wood, metal, or other matter

surveyor: one whose job is to measure land areas

FOR MORE INFORMATION

BOOKS

Murray, Julie. *The Statue of Liberty*. Minneapolis, MN: ABDO Kids, 2017.

National Geographic. *125 Wacky Roadside Attractions*. Washington, DC: National Geographic, 2016.

Prior, Jennifer Overend. *America's Man-Made Landmarks*. Huntington Beach, CA: Teacher Created Materials, 2015.

WEBSITES

Top 10 Famous Landmarks in the World
www.kids-world-travel-guide.com/top-10-famous-landmarks.html
Read about landmarks in other countries.

U.S. National Landmarks
www.mrnussbaum.com/united-states/united_states_landmarks
Check out a map to learn about more US landmarks.

INDEX